786.2.

# Piano Music of
# ROBERT SCHUMANN

EDITED BY CLARA SCHUMANN AND JOHANNES BRAHMS

## Series III

## DOVER PUBLICATIONS, INC.
## NEW YORK

Published in Canada by General Publishing Company, Ltd.,
30 Lesmill Road, Don Mills, Toronto, Ontario.
Published in the United Kingdom by Constable and Company, Ltd., 10 Orange Street, London WC2H 7EG.

*Piano Music of Robert Schumann, Series III*, first published by Dover Publications, Inc., in 1980, contains all the solo piano music from the Collected Works Edition (*Robert Schumann's Werke. Herausgegeben von Clara Schumann*, originally published by Breitkopf & Härtel, Leipzig) not already included in Dover's 1972 volumes *Piano Music of Robert Schumann, Series I* and *Piano Music of Robert Schumann, Series II*. The only items excluded are the earlier versions of Opp. 5, 6, 13 and 14 (only the revised editions of these works are reprinted in the Dover volumes) and the two works, Opp. 56 and 58, for pedal piano (*Pedalflügel*), not playable on a standard piano.

The pieces included in the present volume are from two different sections of the Collected Works Edition: *Serie VII. Für Pianoforte zu zwei Händen* (1879–87), edited by Clara Schumann; and *Serie XIV. Supplement* (1893), edited by Johannes Brahms.

The Table of Contents and Glossary have been prepared specially for the present edition.

The publisher is grateful to the Sibley Music Library of the Eastman School of Music, Rochester, N.Y., for making its material available for reproduction.

*International Standard Book Number: 0-486-23906-3*
*Library of Congress Catalog Card Number: 79-55839*

Manufactured in the United States of America
Dover Publications, Inc.
180 Varick Street
New York, N.Y. 10014

# CONTENTS

# GLOSSARY

OF GERMAN TERMS OCCURRING ON THE MUSIC PAGES

*Belebt, nicht zu rasch:* Animatedly, not too quickly

*Bewegt:* Agitatedly

*Durchaus phantastisch und leidenschaftlich vorzutragen:* To be played throughout with fantasy and passion

*Einfach:* Simply

*Erstes Tempo:* Original tempo

*Etwas bewegter:* Somewhat more agitatedly

*Etwas langsamer:* Somewhat more slowly

*Etwas ruhiger:* Somewhat more calmly

*Etwas schneller:* Somewhat faster

*Im Anfang ruhiges, im Verlauf bewegtes Tempo:* Calm tempo at the beginning, agitated tempo as the piece continues

*Im ersten Tempo:* At the original tempo

*Im lebhaften Tempo:* At a vivacious tempo

*Im Legendenton:* In the tone of a legend

*Im ruhigen Tempo:* At a calm tempo

*Im Tempo:* In tempo

*Kräftig und sehr markirt:* Powerfully, and strongly marcato

*Langsam, (ausdrucksvoll):* Slowly, (expressively)

*Langsam getragen. Durchweg leise zu halten:* Slow and sustained. Keep it soft throughout

*Lebhaft(er):* (More) vivaciously

*Leicht, etwas graziös:* Lightly, somewhat gracefully

*Leidenschaftlicher:* More passionately

*Leise, (innig):* Softly, (fervently)

*L. H. [linke Hand]:* Left hand

*Linke:* Left hand

*Mässig. (Durchaus energisch):* Moderately. (With energy throughout)

*Meine Ruh' ist hin:* "My peace of mind is gone" (quotation from Goethe's *Faust*)

*Mit grosser Kraft:* With great power

*Mit grösster Energie:* With maximum energy

*Mit Kraft und Feuer:* With strength and ardor

*Mit Lebhaftigkeit:* With vivacity

*Mit Ped(al):* With pedal

*Mit zartem Vortrag:* To be played tenderly

*Nach und nach bewegter und schneller:* Gradually more agitatedly and faster

*Nach und nach langsamer:* Gradually more slowly

*Nicht schnell, (leise vorzutragen):* Not fast, (to be played softly)

*Noch rascher:* Even more quickly

*Rasch:* Quickly

*Rechte (Hand):* Right hand

*R. H. [rechte Hand]:* Right hand

*Schnell:* Fast

*Sehr gehalten:* Very sustained

*Sehr kräftig:* With great power

*Sehr markirt:* Strongly marcato

*Sehr mässig:* Very moderately

*Sehr präcis:* Very precisely

*Sehr rasch, mit leidenschaftlichem Vortrag:* Very quickly, played with passion

*Sehr rasch und mit Bravour:* Very quickly and with bravura

*Sehr schnell:* Very fast

*So rasch als möglich:* As quickly as possible

*Tempo des Themas:* Tempo of the theme

*Thema:* Theme

*Verhallend (nach und nach):* Dying away (gradually)

*Viel bewegter:* Much more agitatedly

*Wie vorher:* As before

*Ziemlich bewegt:* Rather agitatedly

*Ziemlich langsam, (empfindungsvoll vorzutragen):* (To be played) rather slowly (and with sentiment)

*zurückhaltend:* Holding back

*Piano Music of*
# ROBERT SCHUMANN

# INTERMEZZI
## für das Pianoforte
### von
# ROBERT SCHUMANN.
### Op. 4.
Kalliwoda gewidmet.

**Presto a capriccio.**

**II.**

III.

Allegro marcato.

attacca 4

# IV.

# V.

# VI.

# IMPROMPTUS
### über ein Thema von Clara Wieck
### für das Pianoforte
### von
# ROBERT SCHUMANN.
#### Op. 5.

# 2.

Lebhafter.

**3.**

Sehr präcis.

**4.**

Ziemlich langsam.

**5.**

Lebhaft.

**6.**

Schnell.

Mit Ped.

# 7.

Tempo des Themas.

# 8.

Mit grosser Kraft.

Mit Ped.

# 9.

# 10.

# Etüden in Form von Variationen
## (Symphonische Etüden)
### für das Pianoforte
#### von
# ROBERT SCHUMANN.
Op. 13. Zweite Ausgabe.

Seinem Freunde William Sterndale Bennett gewidmet.

ETUDE III.

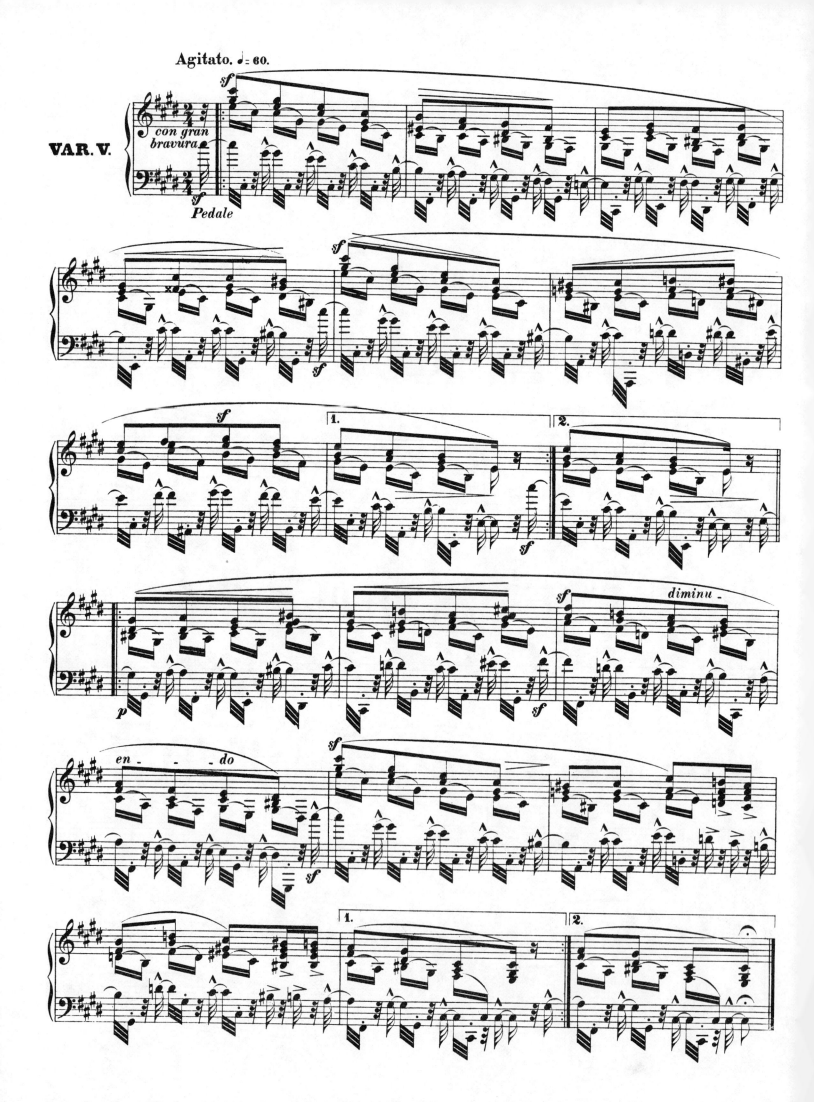

VAR. VII.

sempre marcatissimo
Pedale

**FINALE.**

Allegro brillante. ♩= 66.

# Symphonische Etüden

### für das Pianoforte
### von
# ROBERT SCHUMANN.
#### (Anhang zu Op. 13.)

## Variation I.

Variation II.

# Variation III.

Variation IV.

## Variation V.

# SCHERZO

### für das Pianoforte
### von
# ROBERT SCHUMANN.

(Anhang zu Op. 14.)

# PHANTASIE

für das Pianoforte
von
## ROBERT SCHUMANN.
Op. 17.
Franz Liszt gewidmet.

Motto: Durch alle Töne tönet
Im bunten Erdentraum
Ein leiser Ton gezogen
Für den der heimlich lauschet.
Fr. Schlegel.

Durchaus phantastisch und leidenschaftlich vorzutragen. M.M. ♩=80.

Translation of the motto verse by Schlegel: "In earth's variegated dream, a quiet sustained note sounds through all other notes for those who secretly listen."

Im Legendenton. ♩ = 72.

Erstes Tempo.

Langsam getragen. Durchweg leise zu halten. M.M. ♩.= 60.

# PRESTO
### für das Pianoforte
### von
# ROBERT SCHUMANN.
### (Anhang zu Op. 22.)

Passionato.

# DREI ROMANZEN

## für das Pianoforte
### von
# ROBERT SCHUMANN.
### Op. 28.

Herrn Graf Heinrich II Reuss-Köstritz gewidmet.

Sehr markirt. (M. M. ♩= 88.)

# II.

**Einfach.** ($\quad$ ♪ = 100.)

# III.

**Sehr markirt.** ($\quad$ = 138.)

Etwas langsamer.

Intermezzo 2.

# Scherzo, Gigue, Romanze und Fughette

für das Pianoforte
von
## ROBERT SCHUMANN.
Op. 32.

Fräulein Amalie Rieffel zugeeignet.

## Scherzo.

# Gigue.

**Sehr schnell.** ♩.=116.

# Romanze.

**Sehr rasch und mit Bravour.** ♪ = 144.

# Fughette.

Leise. ♩.= 84.

# VIER MÄRSCHE
## für das Pianoforte
von
# ROBERT SCHUMANN.
## Op. 76.

### I.

**Mit grösster Energie.**

# II.

# III.
## LAGER–SCENE.

Sehr mässig.

Im ersten Tempo.

# IV.

**Mit Kraft und Feuer.**

# DREI PHANTASIESTÜCKE
## für das Pianoforte
### von
# ROBERT SCHUMANN.
### Op. 111.

Frau Fürstin Reuss-Köstritz geb. Gräfin Castell zugeeignet.

# 1.

Sehr rasch, mit leidenschaftlichem Vortrag. M. M. ♩=84.

**2.**

Ziemlich langsam. ♩ = 72.

**Etwas bewegter.**

**Erstes Tempo.**

**3.**

Kräftig und sehr markirt. ♩ = 96.

Mit Pedal.

# ALBUMBLÄTTER
## 20 Klavierstücke
### von
# ROBERT SCHUMANN.
## Op. 124.

Frau Alma von Wasielewski zugeeignet.

## Impromptu.

1832.

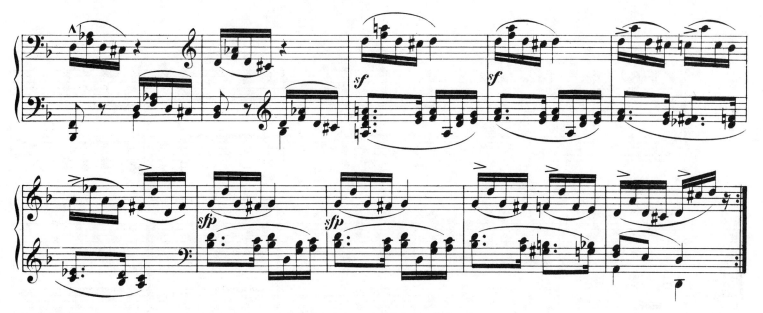

## Leides Ahnung.

1835.

**Langsam.**

N.º 2.

# Scherzino.
### 1832.

**Rasch.**

Nº 3.

# Walzer.
1855.

# Phantasietanz.
### 1836.

**Sehr rasch.**

**No 5.**

# Wiegenliedchen.
1845.

# Ländler.
### 1836.

# Lied ohne Ende.
### 1837.

# Impromptu.

1838.

**Mit zartem Vortrag.**

№ 9.

# Walzer.
### 1838.

**Mit Lebhaftigkeit.**

# Romanze.
### 1835.

# Burla.
1832.

Presto.

№ 12.

**Larghetto.**

1852.

№ 13.

# Vision.
## 1858.

**Sehr rasch.**

**N⁰ 14.**

# Walzer.
### 1852.

**№ 15.**

# Schlummerlied.

1841.

# Elfe.
### 1835.

**So rasch als möglich.**

**No 17.**

*p*

*Mit Pedal.*

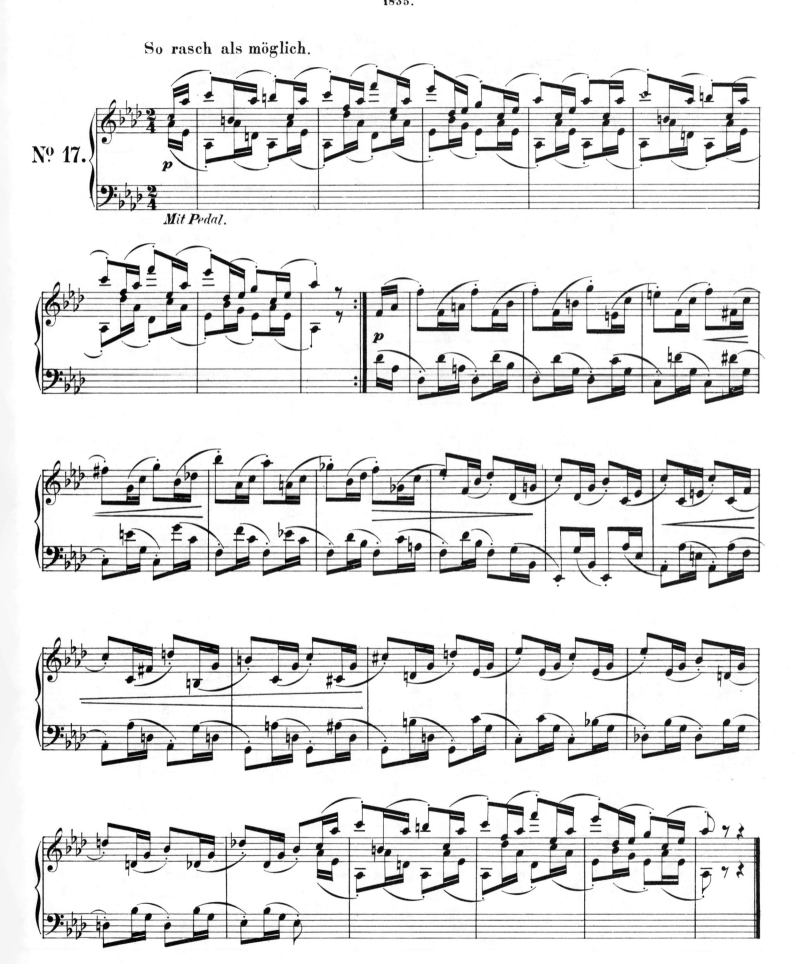

# Botschaft.
### 1838.

Mit zartem Vortrag.

№ 18.

# Phantasiestück.
1859.

Leicht, etwas graziös.

## Canon.
1845.

Langsam.

№ 20.

# Sieben Stücke in Fughettenform

## für das Pianoforte
### von
# ROBERT SCHUMANN.
### Op. 126.

Fräulein Rosalie Leser gewidmet.

## I.

## III.

IV.

Lebhaft. ♩ = 80.

## V.

Ziemlich langsam, empfindungsvoll vorzutragen. ♩ = 54.

# VI.

# VII.

Langsam, ausdrucksvoll. ♪ = 96.

# Gesänge der Frühe
### Fünf Stücke für das Pianoforte
#### von
# ROBERT SCHUMANN.
### Op. 133.
Der hohen Dichterin Bettina zugeeignet.

## I.

## II.

Belebt, nicht zu rasch. ♪ = 190.

# III.

**Lebhaft.** ♩ = 93.

# IV.

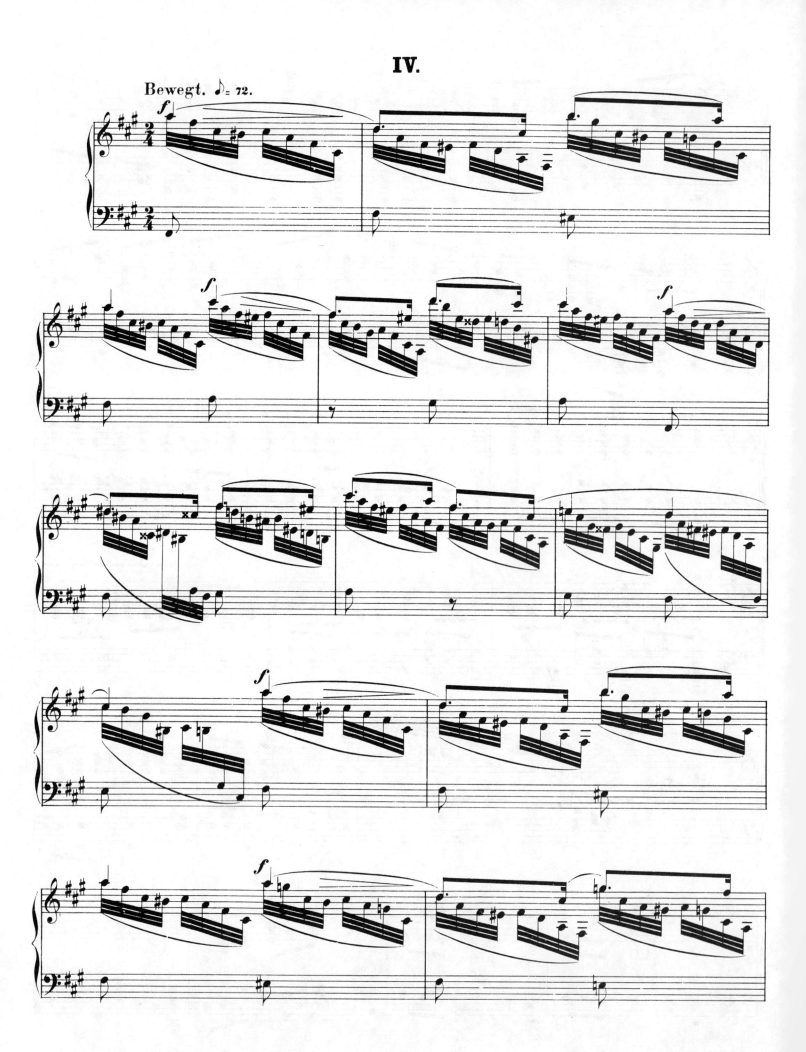

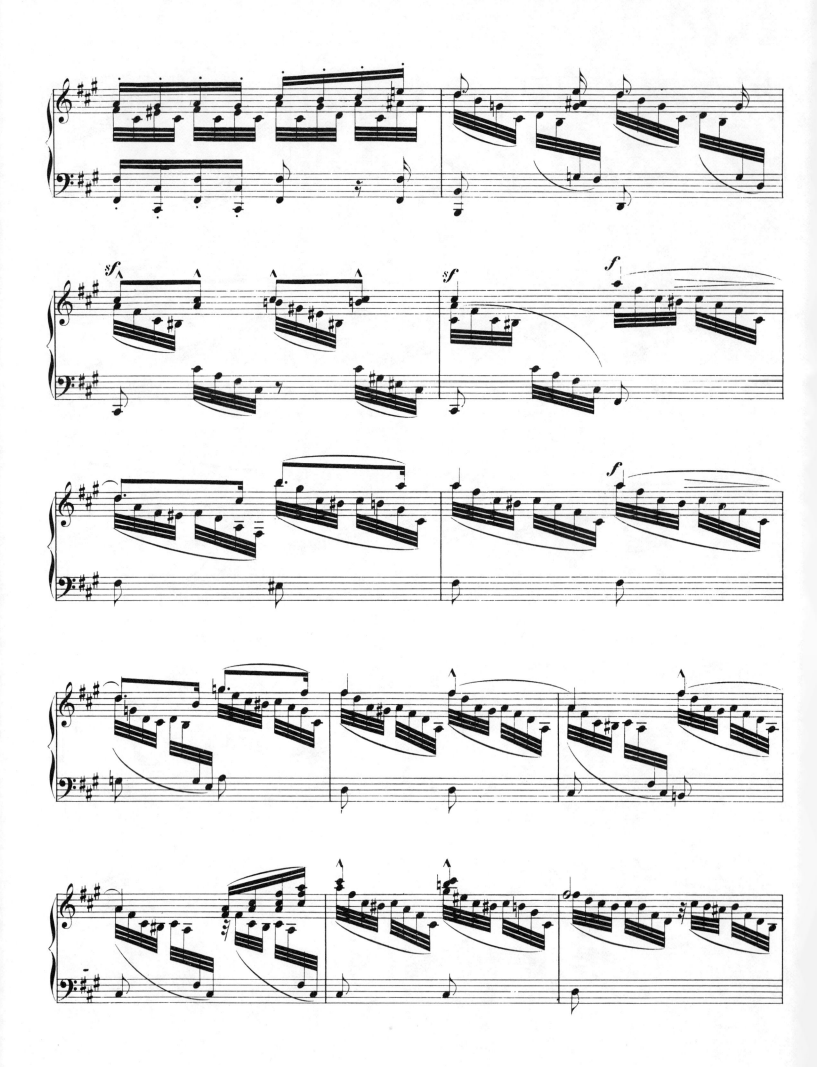

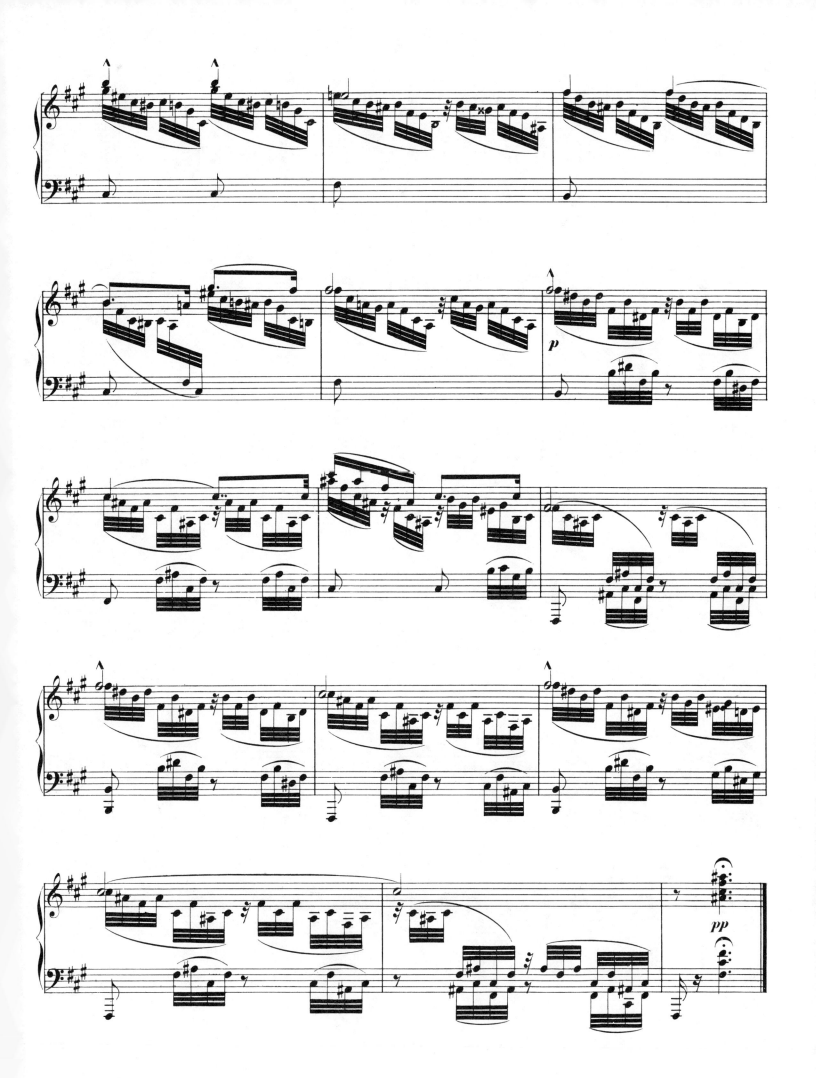

# V.

Im Anfange ruhiges, im Verlauf bewegtes Tempo. ♩ = 68.

# Thema (Es dur)

für das Pianoforte

von

## ROBERT SCHUMANN.

**Thema.**

Leise, innig.